Prayers, Peace and Praise
Guidance for Prayer through Poetry

Poetry from
the Heart Collection
Volume 6

by C. Melita Webb

Prayers, Peace & Praise

Prayers, Peace & Praise

Publisher: Publishing Hearts
Content Editors: Ruth B. Hill and Emogene Price
Copy Editor: Todd Larson
Cover design: RLSather
Chapter art: pixabay.com

Prayers, Peace & Praise

Note to Reader

Every day is a miracle, a blessing, and an incredible opportunity to commemorate the gift of life. One of the best ways to convey our love, gratitude, devotion, and respect to our Heavenly Father is through prayer.

Prayer is a tremendous blessing and a valuable option for all who desire to walk a progressive path of faith. People all over the world pray for various reasons. Whether they may be Catholic, Christian, Muslim, or Jewish, prayer is a vital part of life.

Personally, prayer brings clarity, provides comfort, relieves anxiety, reduces our fears, and directs our focus toward God's will. When we pray, we augment our connection to the still-small voice in our hearts.

Prayer invigorates and empowers us to persevere through challenging moments. For example, we may pray before our airplane takes off and when it begins to land. We may pray before going under anesthesia, and when we wake in recovery.

Most importantly, prayer allows us to communicate privately with our Heavenly Father. What a shower does for the body, prayer does for the mind.

Prayers, Peace & Praise

Dedication
To Seekers of Joy

I dedicate this book to everyone who has endured conflict, trauma, hardship, loss, or pain. Life is not always linear, comfortable, or exciting, though life is a gift and a fantastic miracle. God is the giver of all life, benevolence and grace.

We can encounter favorable situations, periodic obstacles, assorted losses, and grief, as well as other complex outcomes. Our lifestyle and choices may not make sense to our neighbors, family, or friends.

Thankfully, all people have the duty and responsibility to live their best lives. God is the director of life, and our actions need only to please Him.

Occasionally you may encounter opposition, hurdles, or strife. The person offending may not realize the caustic nature of his or her interaction. Other times you may engage someone who covets negativity, lives unhappily or creates conflict, thus may care less about your disposition, feelings, or life.

Keep mentally healthy, and confidently advance in your path of faith. Do not be deterred, stifled, confused, or distracted. When you know that what you are doing pleases God, you must keep marching toward your calling.

Prayers, Peace & Praise

Introduction

Reading the prayers, poems and essays contained in this volume is a great way to relax and invite calmness into your life. Prayer is a beautiful way to focus your thoughts and live a better quality of life.

I will not tell you that prayer settles all situations the way you want. However, God is always in control, and He always works out what is best for us. I can attest that prayer can help you discover what you need.

In the subsequent pages, I share what I know from personal prayer experience and what I comprehend from listening to God's Gospel:

1. Prayer brings you closer to God.
2. Prayer helps you release pain.
3. Prayer cheers up your day.
4. Prayer helps stop tears.
5. Prayer can save your sanity and your life.

One of the best reflections on prayer I ever heard was from best-selling author Iyanla Vanzant: "Every thought is a prayer." Wow, that simple yet profound thought, in many ways, was life-changing for me! Those words deeply convicted my heart and prompted me to clean out the less pleasant thoughts I was wrongly carrying in the rear of my mind.

Continued

The harmony, solace, and affection prayer provides helps me recognize each day as a gift. Prayer does not infer that I have no struggles. It merely signifies that I know I am not alone, God is my redeemer, and I look to God for relief from all afflictions.

As you read this volume, I invite you to write prayers, affirmations, notes, and reflections in the memorandum section. Create personal messages, share your thoughts with God, and increase your joy!

Prayer comforts my soul, relaxes my mind, eases my fears, expunges my stress, and calms me in ways nothing else can. When I pray, God's Spirit helps me analyze my thoughts and concentrate on positivity.

Prayers, Peace & Praise

Contents

Lord, You strengthen me with Your love,
And You comfort me with Your grace.

Prayers, Peace & Praise

Collection Focus Scripture

25 But if we hope for what we do not yet have, we wait for it patiently.
26 In the same way, the Spirit helps us in our weakness. We do not know what we ought to pray for, but the Spirit Himself intercedes for us through wordless groans. 27 And He who searches our hearts knows the mind of the Spirit, because the Spirit intercedes for God's people in accordance with the will of God.
~Romans 8:25-27 (NIV)

Prayers, Peace & Praise

Opening Prayer
What a Perfect God You Are

Dear Father,
What a flawless God You are.
Father, thank you for blessing us
With Your loving peace.
Father, thank you for covering us
With Your mighty power
And Your perfect protection;
And above all else, Father,
Please continue to give us
Your unfailing love
And Your sweet affection.
Father, we love You,
And You are forever
And always worthy of our praise.

Chapter 1
Prayerful Moments of Joy
Showing Gratitude and Speaking Life

Focus Scripture

Blessed are those who have learned to acclaim You, who walk in the light of Your presence, LORD. They rejoice in Your name all day long; they celebrate Your righteousness.
— Psalm 89:15-16 (NIV)

God, the Blessing that You Are

Sweet and adored King,
With You, we have everything.
Because of Your grace,
No need remains unfilled.
No one is orphaned,
Abandoned or alone.
Residing with You
Is the best home.

The Holy Spirit Will Intercede

God is our full defense,
Lasting shelter,
And perfect protector.
Our sins and transgressions
God recalls no more.
As the one true King,
God forgives everything.

Essay of Thought:
God's Daily Peace

Each new day presents excellent opportunities. You can wake with a smile in your heart, pep in your step, and a song of praise on your lips. Having a mind full of gratitude and joy in your soul is an invigorating way to start your day.

How you rise and greet life will set the tone, mood and rhythm for your day. You can positively look at life with an encouraging lens and increase your likelihood of a beautiful day. Count your blessings and embrace your God-given joy.

Choose what you want and what you will allow in your space. Scrutinize the information, media and thoughts you entertain in your mind. Resist negativity, and avoid happiness-destroyers. Protect your inner peace, and remove stress from your life.

Make the essential definitive choice to live a life you love each day. Construct a true vision of how you want to live. Focus your energy on ways that enhance the peace and positivity you desire. Refer to your wishes and select the best options for you and your family.

Prayer:
You Calm Me

Lord, please lovingly soothe me
And help me survive the day.
Please touch my heart,
And console me in Your usual way.
I seek your compassion,
And I crave Your relief.
Father, there is no other way
To survive and thrive than by
Being adorned and insulated
In Your grace.

Essay of Thought:
Speaking to God

When we approach God with our sincere hearts and rational minds, we do not need elaborate words. We need to speak to God as we would lovingly beseech our earthly father with affection, admiration, and honor.

Prayer is not limited to just wealthy, healthy, or prestigious individuals. The poor, homeless, middle-class, and everyone in-between all travel through Jesus on the same path to God. God loves each of His children, and God enjoys the utterances of our sincere hearts and our devotional time spent cultivating our relationship with Him.

Each day, as I walk my journey in mindful ways, I pause and gather God's joy along my way. I envision myself walking by God's side, and this image makes each step more meaningful in my mind. I fill my heart with God's love. By maintaining that goal, my days are brighter. I can smile through my troubles and find calm in the chaos.

No matter where we live, what we have, or how we feel about life, God sees us. God loves and values His children. We are never silent or lost to God.

Prayers:
Seeing Your Blessings

Dear God,
Thank you for everything You do for me.
I now recognize blessings I could not see.
Father, You provide blessed moments
Of silence, serenity, and peace.
Moments required for deeper reflection.
Father, now I comprehend more of
Your desires and intentions for me.

You Saved Me

Father God,
Thank You for never leaving me.
There were many times
The road was rough,
My mind was full of worry,
And my eyes cried tears.
You recognized my struggle,
Reached down,
Pulled me onto my feet,
And saved me.

Learning to Stand

Father, You showed me
How to see your daily
Love and affection for me.
Now I understand
That with You
There is always love
And a place for me.
Through Your eyes I see,
And in Your eyes
I am always worthy.
You stopped the rain,
Made the storm retreat,
And brought me closer to You.
Father, You taught me to stand.

Your Salve of Love

Dear God,
Thank You
For shepherding my soul
Into Your fold.
Veering off Your path
Is disastrous for me.
You filled the void in my spirit,
Calmed my world,
And soothed me
With Your Holy Salve of love.

You Mend My Soul

Father, You cradled me,
Cut away my sorrows
And repaired my soul.
Father, You eliminated my grief
And filled me with
Your love and peace.
Father, You furnished my needs,
Went in-depth,
And brought out
The best in me.

Keep me as the apple of Your eye.
Hide me in the shadow of Your wings.
— Psalms 17:8 (NIV)

Through the Darkness

Dear Father,
Thank you for enveloping me
In Your healing light.
You received me,
Took me by the hand,
Glimpsed deep in my heart,
Listened to my thoughts,
Felt my distress,
And understood my despair.
Father, You heard
Every one of my pleading prayers.
Thank you for bringing
Me through the darkness
And returning me safely
To Your light.

Your Holy Light

Dear God,
Thank you for redeeming me
And returning me to Your garden.
You picked the perfect place
For me to stand.
You touched my heart,
And helped me recognize
That I could enjoy living again.
You saved Your best for me.
Father, You renewed my life
And created options
In spite of my struggles
And beyond the pain.

You Bring Me Joy

Precious Father,
You pulled the curtains,
Opened the windows,
Rekindled my life,
And delighted my flame
With Your sweet joy
To bring meaning to my world.

You raised Your hand,
Pushed back the wind,
And caused the thunder to stop.
You made the mountains move,
Cleared the path
And showed me the best way through,
Safely returning my heart,
Mind and spirit to You.

The Blessing of Prayer

Father God,
Each day we live
To sing praises to You.
Knowing that You
Always listen
Gives us hope, and provides
A genuine sense of security.
Thank you for the gift of prayer.

Your Love is Soothing

Gracious Heavenly Father,
We love and appreciate You.
Everywhere Your Spirit resides
Is full of affection,
Harmony and truth.
Father, we fully surrender
All of our pains, tears,
And struggles to You.

You are Worthy of Our Praise

Father God,
Thank you for bringing
Abounding joy into our hearts.
Father, we genuinely appreciate You.
Each day, our goal is to walk with You
And be worthy of Your grace.
Father, we know that
As long as we are obedient
Your Holy Spirit will direct our way.

God's love is always shining on you.
He stands with you twenty-four hours a day.
You are always covered by His love and His grace.

A Place for Notes

**Chapter 2
Each Day's Beauty
Prayers of Appreciation**

Focus Scripture
*Blessed are those who have learned to acclaim You, who walk
in the light of Your presence, LORD. They rejoice in Your
name all day long; they celebrate Your righteousness.*
— Psalm 89:15-16 (NIV)

Prayerful Reflections:
Nothing is Unseen by You

Dear Beloved Father,

We know that You always see what's going to happen before we even open the door. Before we wake in the morning, our whole day has been blessed by You. Father, Your goodness and Your mercy help us find the strength to stand.

Father, we know that there is nothing unseen to You. You know everything that we will ever encounter. Father, I trust that You have already made our path clear. I know You have already provided for our relief and our rescue.

With You, we have progress, protection, and possibilities. We need nothing else and no one else. Father, we thank you for every day of life, and we send this prayer of appreciation through Your son, Jesus Christ. Amen.

Your Mighty Hand

Dear Father God,

You are the answer to every prayer spoken, every miracle needed, and every deliverance desired. Father, we know that You can accomplish anything, heal anyone, and deliver a miracle, cure or blessing with the slight wave of Your precious and mighty hand. Father, whatever difficulty Your people face, fight or flee today, we ask for You to clear and direct our way.

Father, we already claim whatever we need that aligns us with Your will, enhances our faith, and leads to our victory with You. We send this simple prayer in Your son Jesus' name, amen.

Guide My Way

Dear Loving Father,

Each day You send new wonders and blessings my way. Your beautiful mercy and loving grace will never cease. Father, nothing is as important to me as the plans you have prepared for my life.

I never worry about my day, as I know that You lift me and carry me through each moment. Father, my steps are for You, just as my heart is for You. Please continue to teach me, correct me, and guide me closer to You. Amen.

Tears Fall

Magnificent Father,

My tears keep falling, my heart is aching, and I am lost in all kinds of emotions. I know to lean on You, and I continue to trust You. Yet my tears do not cease. I am not crying for me, but for the people I love and those not yet free.

I cry for those without and those with abundance. Some are suffering, hurt, homelessness, in pain, starving, and perishing, while others are content, prosperous, suffering, and in emotional distress, lost in emotions. Each day I try to be positive, to be of service to You, and to make a difference in Your children's lives. Still, my soul cries out for those in need that I can't reach.

Father, I know You do not need my help, but I pray You continue to send Your beloved ones my way so they can feel Your love and recognize Your grace. I pray this humble prayer through Your Son Jesus' holy name.

Essay of Thought:
Daily Opportunities

Each day is a new opportunity to live your best life. Release everything preventing you from walking in happiness and your purpose.

Free your mind from misery. Release regrets, toxic thoughts, malicious intentions, old battles, aged wounds, and unhealthy relationships. Forgive yourself for prior negative choices.

You learned and matured from every experience. Now that you know better, you can do better. Move forward, release the stress on your heart, mind, body and soul. Accept God's love, forgiveness and grace.

Understand that some people who wronged you may never say they are sorry. Some may not be self-aware enough to realize the harm they caused. Others may not care or may feel justified in their unhealthy behavior. Whatever the case, or cause, let it go.

Do not hold space in your heart for their negativity or carry their pain. Let it all go! Wipe off your feet, release the past, and start a fresh. Commit to being the best possible version of yourself. This is your life, and you must live it well.

Prayers:
Leaning on You

Thank you, God,
For keeping me safe
In Your heart.
Father, there is no place
I would rather be
Than in Your presence
And under Your care.
There is so much more we can do
When we learn to lean on You.

We Give You Praise

Father God, we come
To give You praise.
There is no one else like You.
Every day of life
Is a sweet blessing with You.
Each day we walk with hope
In our hearts because of You.
Our nights are sweeter,
Our joys are greater,
And our sorrows are reduced,
All because of You.
Father, You are our sole hope.

No One is Better than You

God, thank you
For sharing Your heart
And allowing us in Your presence.
Daily, You create a magnitude of blessings.
With You, we lack nothing.
You provide life's nourishing substances,
Aptitudes, and knowledge.
No one is better than You.

Seek God's full light in your world.
May every word that you speak bring glory to His Name.
My every thought of your heart be pleasing to His ears.

The Goodness We Seek

Father God,
You are the goodness we seek.
You are the reason for our smiles,
Even when we have tears.
With you, there is joy
In adversity,
Comfort during the storms,
Calm in the wake of misery,
Bounty in troublesome trial,
Safety in fire,
And wealth in poverty.

Being Your Vessel

Father, please continue
Allowing Your Holy Spirit's
Goodness to flow through me.
Please help me maintain a good heart.
I desire to be a good
And favorable vessel for You.

Loving Father

Dear God,
Thank You for all You
Continue to do for me.
I now recognize many more
Blessings I was unable to see.
Loving father, I now understand
More of Your wishes, desires,
And purpose for my journey.
Thank You again for all
You have done for me.

You Give Me Power

God, when I pray to You,
I am refreshed and renewed.
Father, You give me hope,
Love, peace, and strength.
You do so much more
Than anyone else could ever do.
You provide the power
For me to make it through my day.
I think of Your promises
And Your loving heart.
My heart overflows with joy.

God is the source of all power.

Our Safe Harbor

Father God, thank You
For being our safe harbor.
There is no place
We can get so lost
That You cannot care for us
And retrieve us
To Your safety and comfort.
I am thankful that even
When we fail to see options,
You have what we need.

Your Strength is My Safety

Father, there is a special place
Deep in our heart reserved for You.
The human eye cannot see it,
And man cannot manipulate it.
Father, it only belongs to You.
It's where I hear Your words,
Feel Your love, sense Your blessing
And rest in Your comfort.
Your strength is my safety.
I am delighted
To worship You.

Help Me Be More Like You

Dear God,
Please continue to touch me
With Your incredible power,
Your unforgettable mercy
And Your precious grace.
Please help me see the blessing
In my storms,
And the safety
In Your peace.
Please anoint me
With more of Your love,
And continue to be
The power of my life.
Please help me
Be more like you.

Please Guide Our Steps

Dear God,
We come before Your
As Your humble servants
Asking that You increase our knowledge
And our understanding of Your word.
Father, please amplify the skills we need
To live each day as You desire.
Please guide our hearts,
Steer our minds
And move our hands
So that we best serve You.
Father, please direct our steps
So that we always bring peace,
Speak your truth,
And glorify
Your Holy name.

You Are Always the Answer

Father, You are always
The answer to our prayers.
We appreciate everything
You continue to do.
We remain in awe of You.
Thank you for bringing me
Through the storms of life,
And steering me
Onto the right path.
I look forward
To living in Your love,
And walking in Your peace
Every day.

The Ultimate Provider

Father God,
You are our Supreme Provider.
Father, the King of Kings
And the Lord of Lords.
Your words are our fortress.
Your peace is our shield.
We are thankful for You.
Your unlimited wisdom
Is enlightening and true.
Your judgment is always right.
There is no light or hope
When You are absent from our life.

Give thanks to the Lord, for He is good.
His love endures forever.
— Psalm 107:1

Food for Our Soul

Thank you, God,
For snatching us
From the grips of the enemy
And drawing us safely
Into Your arms.
We celebrate
Every moment in Your presence.
Your utterances are like
The air we need to breathe
And the restorative water
We need to drink.
Thank you for continuously
Delivering vital food
For our minds, bodies, and souls.

We Lift Your Name

Father God,
We commemorate Your love,
And we sing Your praise.
Even in our state of hurt,
Confusion, and grief,
We choose to honor You
And to lift Your Holy Name.

Father God, thank you
For the gift of life
And the multitude of blessings
You provide each day.

Chapter 3:
The Blessing You Are in Christ
Essays and poems

Focus Scripture

He will again have compassion on us, And will subdue our iniquities. You will cast all our sins Into the depths of the sea.
— Micah 7:19 (NKJV)

Essay of Thought:
Seeing God's Blessings

Watch for the blessings God is sending to you. When they come your way, step up and take the position God aligned with your life. If you refuse to embrace and live the dreams God gives you, He will give them to someone else: the ideas you did not complete, the business you never started, or, in my case, the life lessons book I did not publish.

The work God wants to be accomplished will be completed, regardless of our denial, failures, and missed opportunity. It is up to us to see how we best fit into God's plan and wishes for our lives. Your time has not passed. You are still here, you have a purpose and an opportunity to experience your best life. You can always use your life for God and His joy.

Poems:
God Can Heal Your Heart

When your heart hurts
And feels like it's splitting in two,
Know that you are not alone.
With one-touch or wave
Of His mighty hand,
God can heal your heart.
With one motion.
God can destroy your sorrow,
Blow away your tears,
And bring joy
Back into your life.

> *Every life has a purpose*
> *And every breath you take matters.*
> *Choose to fully embrace*
> *The beauty of your life.*

God is King

As a beloved child of the King,
You are worthy of your dreams.
You are part of God's beloved royal family,
And He treasures you completely.
You have been made new.
You were chosen, released, redeemed,
Transformed, blessed, and anointed
For His purpose.
Your past has been forgiven.
You are healed, loved, and protected
By God's unfailing love, mighty power,
And amazing grace.

Sharing Christ's Love

As followers of Christ,
We must walk in His loving ways.
We should leave everyone
That we meet with traces
Of God's goodness and His grace.
We should greet each other
With a smile on our face
And take time to enjoy
The blessing of each other's company.
There is only love in Christ,
And there should only be love in us.

Essay of Thought:
Facing Life, Finding Peace

Sometimes you have to accept life's challenges, trials and difficulties as they are. It doesn't mean that you are content or unworthy or do not want better for yourself. It just means you are grateful for the life God has given you.

When we slow down, step back, and take a good view of our lives, we can see the joys as well as the pain. We can recall good times, great memories, and wonderful moments of happiness and peace. We may find comfort on rainy days by acknowledging that sunny days will offset the clouds and the rain. Understand and believe that most trials and troubles do not last forever.

One of the best ways to bring more joy into your life is by helping someone in need. Even when we are not doing as well as we would like, often we still have more than others in our communities.

Strive to achieve God's full vision and harmony for your life. Take a self-assessment, be candid about your situation, and identify what you can realistically do to improve your life. Make the best out of your circumstances, and decide to find joy even when you are struggling. Perhaps by changing your life view, you can uncover the blessings in the rain.

Poem
Embrace Your Life Each Day

Wake and embrace the life
In your God-given day.
Bring God your full enthusiasm.
Greet each moment
With a heart full of joy and faith.
Choose to interact in the world
As God would today.
Meet each other with an open heart,
A warm smile and a kind attitude.
Be happy, encouraged, and thankful.
For God has given you
A new blessing today.

Essays of Thought:
God Loves You As You Are

There is never a reason to compare your life to that of anyone else. God took great care and gifted each of us with own unique journey and walk of faith. Even identical twins have different gifts, dreams, talents and aspirations. They may have many similarities, but one may love science and the other may excel in math.

Shine in Your Own Way

What I choose to like is based on my thoughts, desires, and preferences. What you decide to like is based on your individual opinions, desires, and preferences. I may love the sunshine, and you may love the moonlight. Neither the sun nor the moon is more important in God's eyes; they just have different responsibilities, functions, uses, and other times to shine in their own way.

Walk Your Own Path in Joy and Peace

Just as God created each of us for our own path, the sun has its course, and the moon has its system. The flowers have always had an incredible variety of colors, scents, and times to bloom. That, too, is part of God's plan. Our job is to wake up each day and find a way to walk our faith path in joy and peace.

Continued

You Are a Unique Flower in God's Garden

My steps may never cross your path, yet we are both here for the same reason. When we lose sight of our uniqueness and God's direction, we can become sad or stressed, or we may give in to the pressures of society.

You are like one of the flowers in God's beautiful garden. You will grow in your own way each day. Your beauty and your purpose are not diminished when another person shines. In God's eyes, your life is just as bright as that of the person standing next to you.

Shine Your Light Bright Each Day

Choose to live each day shining your light and never standing in anyone's shadow. Take your next step, your next breath, and the next chance to live your best life. As we grow and mature, we come to understand the truth that everyone's life has value, purpose, and a reason to be grateful.

Accept Life as the Blessing That it Is

I accept my life as the blessing that it is. Even with my challenges and struggles, I am thankful to be alive. I invite you to accept your life as the blessing that you are.

Poems
The Creator of Goodness

Our beloved Father
Is the God of all wisdom, justice,
Mercy and peace.
He is the Creator of everything good,
Including the sun, the moon,
And the air that we breathe.
There is never any wrong found
In Him or His miraculous deeds.
Feel safe and secure knowing
That, as you proceed,
God is providing
For your needs.

Only You Can Stop Your Shine

You are so amazing, and only
You can stop your shine.
Believe in yourself and know
That, with God,
You live your best life.
My child, stand firm,
Stay tuned into My presence,
And always listen to Me.
When you are in doubt, remain quiet.
Keep My word in your heart
And mind at all times.
Remain calm.
Together, we will weather the storm.

My mouth shall speak of wisdom;
And the meditation of my heart
Shall be understanding.
— Psalms 49:3

Essay of Thought:
You Are Enough

Right now, and at this minute, we are enough. Often we get so distracted during our days that we lose track of time. We can become frustrated and open ourselves up to feelings of gloom, anxiety, and even occasional sadness.

Today, my health challenges require me to be still. During the stillness, I find energy, strength, answers, and clarity to issues I have been trying to clear from my heart and mind all week.

I have no voice, so I just smile, look up, and say, "Thank you, God." I nod, raise my hands in praise, and realize that God only wants what we are capable of giving. It does not matter that my breathing is off or that my eyes are swollen. It only matters that I have a pure heart for God.

Wow! Isn't that something? Blind people do not see as sighted people do; God still loves them. Mute people cannot praise the way verbal people can. You know what? God still loves them, too!

So, no matter what trials hinder you in life, God will always love you. I felt such a weight lift off my mind and my spirit. I realized that not every question or problem has an answer I can figure out.

Continued

No matter how much I want to fix the world, I cannot. I can only send love into the world, and so can you! What is important is that we show up in life every day with determination, love, and a commitment to God. Everything else will work itself out.

God Always Makes a Way

Rest assured that God
Always looks out for you.
Even when you cannot see,
He is directing you.
When you cannot hear,
He is listening for you.
When your mind is confused
And your way seems unclear,
Calm your heart.
Trust God and His power.
Nothing gets past
God's watchful eye,
Loyal heart, or sturdy hand.
God always shelters you.

Centering Prayer
My Faith in You

Sweet, beloved Father,
Only You know the extensive facts
And dimension of our battles.
Thankfully, You discern the depth
Of our pain and suffering.
Thank You for setting into motion
The ending to our tears and pain.
Father, it is because of You
That we can fight and stand.
The pressures of the world
Are no match for our love,
Devotion, and faith in You!

Place your focus on the one
who loves you and cares for your soul.
Pleasing God is always our ultimate goal.

Prayers:
You Are Everything

Gracious Father,
You are everything we seek.
You are the loving creator
Of the air we breathe.
You are the ultimate provider
Of the food we eat.
Your oceans, lakes, streams,
And rivers provide abundantly.
Your sky, trees, plants, berries,
And every earthly thing,
Provide a gracious table
Of life-giving substance.

Precious Creator

Dear Precious Creator,
As I think of Your goodness,
I instinctively close my eyes,
And harmony fills my mind.
Father, thank You for Your love and grace.
Father, You made the ultimate sacrifice
To ensure our future in peace.
Father, Your comfort
Brings a smile to my soul
And warms my heart.
Your love is soothing to our souls.

Poem
God is Our Refuge

God is our refuge, shelter,
Oasis, and source of power.
God provides our sustenance,
Comfort, and strength.
We have no need that God cannot fill.
We have no illness that God cannot heal.
We have no sorrow that God cannot remove.
We have no pain that God cannot eliminate.
God is a very present help to us each day.

Prayer
Surrender Your Struggles

Dear Heavenly Father,
Thank You for walking with me
And blessing each day.
Father, Your spirit resides with me,
Guides and balances my life.
You brace me as I stumble,
Ensuring my safety.
You are a loving and merciful God.
Father, with you, I smile, walk softly,
And celebrate each day.

Poem
Grasp the Love of God

Grasp tightly
To the glory of God
And keep His will,
And you will be all right.
Do not entertain anger,
Discord, hate, malice,
Or any thoughts of strife.
As the beloved child of the King,
You can rest, rejoice, and report.
For God is in control,
And He will always
Make things right.

A Place for Your Notes

Chapter 4:
Being a Warrior of God
Living in Peace

Focus Scripture
You did not choose me, but I chose you and appointed you so that you might go and bear fruit—fruit that will last—and so that whatever you ask in my name the Father will give you.
— John 15:16 (NIV)

Poems
Please Guide Our Steps

Beloved child of God,
No one can replace or displace you
In your Heavenly Father's eyes.
God nurtured you before birth.
Stop, and recognize your worth.

God designed your life
And guaranteed your victory.
You will not be defeated
By circumstance unless
You renounce your birthright.
Consider your destiny and pray
For strength on your journey.

A Joyful Life

Commit to living a joyous life.
Free your mind, body, and energy
Of every adverse effect, poor intention,
And negative reaction,
Then pick up a shield
Of peace and satisfaction.
Dismiss your worry
And expel your fear.
Only acknowledge positivity,
And more positivity will be near.

Hold tightly to the love of God, and
trust that you will be all right.

Pray Your Path Clear

Whenever stress or anxiety
Tries to dominate me,
I focus my energy on God.
Meditating on God's goodness
Calms my heart,
Erases distressing thoughts,
And refreshes my soul.
I know that God never fails.
I am never alone,
And God remains on the throne.

Prayer
Love, Harmony, and Truth

Dear Beloved Father,
We joyfully stand with You
In faith, love, and truth.
Father, we devote our lives
To honoring and praising You.
Nothing transpires
That You cannot control.
We are eternally
Obedient to You.
Your Spirit delivers
Love, harmony, and truth.

Trust God's Perfect Timing

Walk in ways to navigate
Closer to the Spirit of God,
And God's essence
Will be nearer to you.
Commit to live in God's peace
And walk exclusively in God's grace.
Persist in steadfast faith.
Hope is a prayer away.
Be faithful, honest, and true.
Trust God's timing, and believe
That God will work everything out for you.

The Strength of Your Faith

Exude peace,
Exercise tolerance,
And facilitate love.
Every action you initiate
And every journey you make
Indicates the strength of your faith.
Trust that a subtle adjustment
To intentions and expectations
Will result in better communication.

Meet the World with Love

No matter what you experience,
Each day is a blessed gift
And a unique opportunity for you.
How you choose to perceive the world
Reflects on you.
Therefore, aspire to be
What you wish to see.
Greet the world
With a generous smile,
And demonstrate
Compassion and unity.

You Never Walk Alone

Never mistrust God's affection for you.
God knows all, beholds all,
And He can rectify all.
There is nothing God cannot achieve.
Continue to petition prayerfully
For God's grace and maintain zealous faith.
God's Holy Spirit insulates you
From the final fall.

Life is Proof of God's Love

Beloved child of God,
Your existence is evidence of God's love.
God's kindness should flow
From your presence.
Embrace your life
And accept God's grace.
Welcome God's love
And enjoy His embrace.
God is with you every day.

God's Strength and Light

God transmits precise strength,
Energy, and courage for each day.
Never impose a limit
On God's blessings, His Glory,
Or the development of your faith.
Stretch your soul,
and grow in knowledge.
Remain available to the fullness
Of God's glorious light
And behold, sweet deliverance.

Master of Peace

Be a master of peace
And a soldier for God.
Live each day zealously.
Let your actions show your faith.
Be authentic to yourself
And live in honor.

Continue to mature daily
In faith, love, and knowledge.
God will continue to supply
Your love and power.

I Am Everything

I am everything you seek.
I can fill your desire
And resolve every need.
I am the supreme Creator
Of every good thing.
Every battle you encounter
Is a moment in time.
Some moments are sad.
Other times are uneventful,
Flying quickly by
The unassuming eye.
Take heed, as most moments are sweet.
Wait in good cheer for one day
You will reside with Me
In a joyful life for entirety.

Continue Trusting Me

My devoted child,
You are never alone.
Even in the darkest hours,
I am near your devoted heart.
Evade distractions, and stay
Aware of the enemy's actions.
He is seeking
To destroy your soul.
Call out to Me
If you fear, stumble, or fall.
Trust Me, your beloved King.
I am never wrong.

Let God Lead Your Way

Each day, our goals
Are to walk in God's grace,
Shine brightly against
The world's darkness,
And grow stronger in our faith.
We are not required to
Know all the answers,
Learn every scripture by heart,
Or need "special words" to say.
We must simply remain obedient,
And God will lead our way.

Essay of Thought:
God is Cheering for You

Each day is part of an ongoing lesson. Our ability to learn is one of God's many blessings on us. Each lesson is designed to help you mature and progress in your purpose. Lessons may include moments of joy, peace, happiness, challenge, growth, and sometimes sadness.

Life can periodically knock you off your feet, hit you in your face, and keep you down if you let it. The crucial key is our faith and reliance on God. Getting back up, dusting off the troubles, and finding ways to keep progressing indicates that we have passed the lesson.

Understand that you cannot afford to give up or give in on your life. Defeat is not how our victory ends. It is not in our destiny. It does not matter if you are age 15, 50, or 90.

God has plans for your happiness and your victory. So please do not give in to an unhappy or unfulfilled life. Do not think or choose to feel that your best years are behind you. Find more reasons and figure out ways to keep enjoying life, get back up, and keep making life work. God is always cheering for you.

Poem
Remain Focused

Are you laser-focused
On what God wants you to do,
Or are you becoming distracted
By the things the world
Is pushing toward you?
You must continue to be laser-tuned
Into what God wants for you.

If you become distracted,
Stop and be still.
Say a small prayer,
And allow God's Spirit
To guide you to what
God has called you to accomplish.

Shine brightly against the world's darkness.
You may never know how many people
You help each day with your smile.

Essay of Thought:
God Has Your Victory

No matter what is going on in your day, you will always remain one of God's brightest stars. Your struggles do not define you. Your illness, challenges, impairment, and disabilities do not make you any less important to God. Even the things you may not like about yourself do not matter to God. God will always love you as you are.

The trials you come up against may seem insurmountable. That is part of the enemy of our souls' plan. He wants to distract and confuse us so that we stumble. You must remember: you are built to survive. Your resilience is in your soul.

Those distractions and challenges are only a portion of your story, a small chapter in the book of life God has planned for you. So choose to wake up each day and shine through the pain, the sadness, and the trouble. You are worthy of all the joy your heart can hold. Remember that God has your victory planned.

Poem
A Warm, Joyful Heart

Dedicated child of God,
Keep calmness as the center
Of your life, and hold onto
The goodness in your heart.
Manifest good thoughts
In your mind at all times.
Never release yourself from
The knowledge of God.
Stand firm in your purpose,
And be true to your faith.
Walk each day in kindness and love.
Continue to praise God above.

Seek God's full light in your world.
May every word that you speak bring glory to His Name.
My every thought of your heart be pleasing to His ears.

A Place for Notes

**Chapter 5:
Living in God's Love
Focusing on Positivity**

Focus Scripture

16 And I will ask the Father, and he will give you another advocate to help you and be with you forever— 17 the Spirit of truth. The world cannot accept him, because it neither sees him nor knows him. But you know him, for he lives with you and will be[a] in you.
John 14:16-17

Poem
My Dear

Do not rush, be patient,
And wait for My touch.
Place your focus on Me.
As your Divine Creator,
I am all that you need.
Imagine the most beautiful thing
That you have ever seen.
That is what you are to Me.

Prayer of Release
Blessed Miracles Each Day

Father God,
You perform infinite miracles,
And I trust You to safeguard my day.
When I find myself in puzzlement
Or confusion, my heart calls to You.
I listen for Your Spirit and try
To interpret the gentle pulls
Of my soul.
Only You can seize the hurt
And banish my pain.

Prayer
You Fulfill My Needs

For You fulfill my every need.
You help me survive
When I am lost
And redirect my world.
When I cannot see,
You tenderly shepherd me.
Father, when I don't think
I can take another step,
You provide my energy.
There is no one better than You!

Poems
Choose

Choose life
By placing God first
In your life.

Choose peace
By opening your heart
And welcoming God's serenity in.

Choose joy
By willingly accepting
God's love, guidance and direction.

God Can Fix It

When your world feels unsteady
And your tears continuously drop,
Be still, close your eyes
And take time to pray.
Give God your worries,
Pain, fear, and grief.
God will sturdy your feet,
Calm your mind,
And bring balance
Back into your life.

Essay of Thought:
You Are Fabulous

You are fabulous! You, yes you. You get up each day and give your best effort to God, life, your family, and yourself. You keep trying, keep going and getting back up for the glory of God.

God never asks more from us than we can achieve. I believe that God knows there is more in us than we may realize or accept; that we can be stronger, love harder, act wiser, and walk closer to Him.

Our struggles never come from God. Our challenges, pain and suffering come from the enemy of our soul and sometimes from the choices we make through our free will. Even then, God remains by our side.

We may think we have sinned too hard or too deep, been too wrong, not listened to God, been away from embracing our calling, and many other thoughts that can block us from seeing and feeling our full connection with God.

Never let your spirit be so weighed down by hurt, guilt, or shame that you think you have lost God's love, connection or affection. That will never happen. God wants the best for each of us. He will continue to reach out and send His love to you.

Continued

I think that as long as we make consistent efforts and heartfelt progress, God will see our intentions are pure. Then He adds His strength to us so that we can achieve things for His glory and our betterment in Him. So keep going and know that God is with you. Never forget how deeply God cares for you!

Prayers
God is Near

Dear Heavenly Father,
No matter how difficult my day,
You wrap me with Your love
And show me the route
To keep my spirit fixed on You.
You repair my mishaps
In the most beautiful ways.
Because of Your constant help,
I realize I have nothing to fear,
And more importantly,
I know You are near.

God's Holy Spirit is Near

When you choose to trust God
And believe in His almighty power,
You will experience
A new sense of freedom.
You will have smiles and joy,
Even during your toughest challenges.
You will find ways to walk in peace
While others struggle in chaos.
You trust that God's Holy Spirit
Is always with you,
And you know that you
Will never take another step alone.

Rise and Shine

Rise and shine.
Get prepared to enjoy your day.
Each step you make
Should be grounded in faith.
Keep your eyes
On the coveted prize:
Your life.
Ignore the world's attempts
To dissuade you from living
A God-centered life.
Walk strong in your purpose.
Live firm in your faith,
And walk confidently in God's grace.

The Joy of Being Alive

Beautiful one,
Remember who you are.
God loves you, and to God,
Your destiny is brighter than any star.
Release the concerns from your day.
Let all pains and pressure fade away.
Let nothing block your smile
Or the joy you feel from being alive.

Trust that You Are Fine

Our sweet and loving
Heavenly Father
Is phenomenal, generous and kind.
All of God's children
Are always on His mind.
He loves and cares for each one
Every day,
And in His special way
Your life is always
Of utmost importance to God.

Your Thoughts & Prayers

Your Thoughts & Prayers

Remain patient and calm. God stands with you during every storm.

A Place for Notes

Chapter 6:
Calming the Mind Before Sleep
Prayers of Gratitude

Focus Scripture

For I am the LORD your God who takes hold of your right hand and says to you, Do not fear; I will help you.
— Isaiah 41:13 (KJV)

Prayers
It is an Honor to Serve You

Dear God,
As we prepare to close
Our eyes for the evening,
We want to thank You
For another blessed day of life.
Father, we want to thank You
For the sun, moon, wind, and the rain.
Father, with You,
Every day is a blessing.
Each breath we breathe is a miracle.
Every step we take
Is an unmatched opportunity,
Father, it is consistently an honor
And a privilege to serve You.

You Make Our Day

Father God,
As we shut our eyes tonight,
We thank You for another glorious day
Of your sweet, precious blessings.
Father, we know it was You
Who carried us through
Each step we made today.
Father, we thank You for continuing
To send You loving kindness
And blessings our way.

Your Goodness and Sweet Mercy

Dear God,
As we release the day
And begin to embrace
A beautiful night of sweet rest,
We thank You for the precious gift of today.
Father, we thank You
For meeting our needs,
Looking past our shortcomings,
And caring for us and our loved ones.
We appreciate Your loving compassion,
Tender guidance, and supreme wisdom.
Father, thank You for allowing us
Your divine goodness and sweet mercy
Every day.

We Come to Praise You

Father God,
We come to thank You.
We come to give You praise.
Even in our hurt, confusion, and grief,
We choose to honor Your holy name.
Father, through our tears, illness,
Sadness, pain, and other infirmaries
We know that You are the only answer
And the only real relief.

Guidance and Forgiveness

As you close your eyes,
Take a few minutes to pray.
Give God thanks for every
Blessing in your day.
Ask God for forgiveness
If by chance you went astray.
Ask for His continued guidance,
And He will lead your way.

United Prayer for Peace

Dear Magnificent Father,
Please continue to touch our lives each day
With Your love, power, grace, and generosity.
Father, I have no other intention
Then to do Your will
And honor Your name each day.
Father, I know You always know our needs
Before we are aware of the concern.
Father, I ask you to look out
And continue to bless the world
With Your kindness, comfort, and grace.
Father, I pray that everyone
Will come to know Your peace,
Acknowledge Your powers
And yield to Your ways.
Father, may we have peace today.

Poem
Relax Your Mind

Make time to rest
So you can feel your best.
Relax all of your cares away.
Smile and reflect on all
Of the beautiful moments
God placed into your day.
Close your eyes
And bring your focus
To your energy and peace.
Pray and send all worry, stress,
Anxiety and tension away.
Do not permit your mind to stray.
Stay focused on God's Peace.

Hold on and trust
That God has made provisions
And a better path for you.

Prayer
Fortify My Life

Father, please fortify my life
And accept all my love for You.
Father, please lead and direct me;
Help me stay on the correct path
Of Your life-giving truth.
Please allow me a relaxed
And soothing night
As I rest my head, close my eyes,
And concentrate on Your guiding light.
Thank You for Your flawless love
Which surrounds me morning,
Noon, and night.

Amen.

Special Reader Note:

Please make sure to enjoy every moment of your day. Block out anything that causes you stress, hardship, or pain. God designed you to live in peace and harmony. Nothing but joy should come your way!

Keep going forward toward your victory. Realize that no two paths are ever the same, nor will our strides be identical.

Be true to yourself, and stand firm in your love for God. Listen when He speaks in your heart, and stay the course He has outlined for you.

Closing Thoughts:
Accept the Master's Plan

Eliminate all negative emotions, disagreeable opinions, sad memories, and questionable agendas from your mind. Fight back against the negative dreams and scary nightmares.

Beware of the pessimistic people in your environment; do not accept their negative energy, desires, or motivation. Acknowledge that you understand their agenda and that it doesn't align with your God-given purpose. More than likely you have helped them all your life—and, in some cases, to your own detriment.

Stand up and rebuke the disturbing problems and circumstances in your life. Block their continued choice to languish in misery and all of their attempts to share it with you or bring it into your environment. You must protect your mind, heart, and spiritual life. Admonish them and their chosen situations.

Clear away what you do not need in your life and make way for more of the goodness, increased happiness, and the additional joy God is sending into your life.

Do not hold any space in your heart or mind for old hurts, stale misery, ancient sorrow, previous tension, anxiety, or fear about what tomorrow will bring. Your job is to believe in the goodness and glory of God.

Continued

Choose to joyfully step into your freedom, as it is
close at hand. Remember, your blessings are
already included in the Master's plan.

Closing Prayer
The Sweetest Love

Father, You are
The sweetest love I know.
Each day You gently catch me
As I stumble, and You
Support and assist me.
You are invariably protecting
Me from the fall.
You make sure I softly land.
You fix my world with Your care,
Kindness, and affection.
I appreciate having time
And a special place with You.

Thank you

Please take a few moments to leave a review on the site where you purchased this copy. Your thoughtful and accurate review of this collection will help others find books to enjoy and share.

In addition, your thoughts will be a great help to the author.

Thank you for sharing part of your journey with us.

Please be sure to check out our website and follow our blog at www.cmelitawebb.com

Poetry from the Heart Collection
By C. Melita Webb

In these dark and challenging times, we all need more light. I turn to God and allow Him to be my guide. My life compels me to live in peace and walk in the spirit of love. Often I pray, and God answers through a lesson or the still small voice in my heart. It is out of those moments of devotion that my poetry is written.

All is Redeemed in Truth and Light, was published at my father's request; it contains precious bits of my heart and guided me back to the beginning of light. Five encouraging poetic chapters of life's journey and heartfelt sentiments of faith spurred by love, loss, grief, and the death of people I have loved my whole life. It was my soul's first awakening.

The Light That is You, outlines my vision of emotional development and my view of the next generation's struggle. At that writing, I realized we are all light in this world. We are all capable, and we need to believe we are essential to God. He wants us to live happily and to believe in our value.

Continued

God Placed You Here, is our motivational powerhouse. An encouraging book full of short purposeful nuggets of affirmations and empowering sentiments of faith is a reader favorite. This delightful book reinforces who we are in God's eyes.

Built for God's Glory, is a volume of profound thoughts and reflections. Poetry and prayers crafted around extended essays and topics we may encounter in life.

God's Guiding Light of Peace, is our series strongest comforter. This expansive volume is structured to encourage calm, decreases heated emotions, and soothe anxiety. When difficult situations obstruct the clarity of our heart or purpose, these words of faith direct our mind and energy back to God's light

About the Author

C. Melita Webb is a lover of life who is visually challenged. She has loved words and books all her life. As a student, she excelled in writing deeply touching and reflective prose.

Publishing was a dream she gave up on 30+ years ago, though she continued to write in her heart, mind, and spirit. Later, she began to speak and write into the hearts of her family and friends, too.

In fact, it was at the request of a loved one that the first book in her Poetry from the Heart collection was published. She had no idea how powerful her words would still be, or how many had longed to find a voice like hers.

Her writings are full of passion, clarity and purpose. They span many years and phases of life. Each book in her collection tells a story of love, life, and humanity. Included are reflective poems, loving affirmations, supportive prayers, motivational essays, and cries from the heart. She writes the words that live in all our hearts.

Prayers, Peace, and Praise, is a perfect gift for you and anyone you want to encourage and inspire. Please enjoy this collection with our love and best wishes.

— The Poetry from the Heart team

Social connections and places you can find us on the internet.

Feel free to email us at cmelitawebb@aol.com

Visit our website at www.cmelitawebb.com
See our reviews at goodreads.com

All additional social media links to our YouTube channel and inspirational podcast are available on our website.

We hope you enjoyed this time with us, and we look forward to connecting with you soon.

Sincerely,

The Poetry from the Heart team

**Other Poetry from the Heart books
by C. Melita Webb**

God's Guiding Light of Peace:
Strength to Stand Through Life's Storms
August 2019

Built for God's Glory:
Understanding Our Purpose
March 2018

God Placed You Here:
A Walk of Faith
August 2017

The Light That is You:
A Conversation of God's Love
October 2016

All is Redeemed in Truth and Light
Poetry from the Heart
July 2016

Please visit us at *www.cmelitawebb.com*

www.ingramcontent.com/pod-product-compliance
Lightning Source LLC
LaVergne TN
LVHW011356080426
835511LV00005B/314